Adam Cannot Be Adam, Kelli Anne Noftle's "quixotic and visionary" second book, unfolds and unfolds a fresh consciousness out of her personally mythologized logic. Inside a linguistic "circle of white noise" where the double bind, the double personae of the self resides, you'll find a lively physics of invention. Noftle's dream play of this "story" of two Adams echoes Valéry's philosophical mix between seeing and forgetting / remembering, between apples and oranges, between "thirst and indifference." The book's declarative stance offers us a stunning variation on the normative pose of speaking agency. Noftle's unique diction is the perfect habitat to breed her wild visual taxonomy. It is a work of art, interrupted by light—a luminous "engine to a doppelganger," a desolation of beauty blown in on the paradox of the future.

ELENA KARINA BYRNE, AUTHOR OF *SQUANDER*

William James tells us, "We ought to say a feeling of and ... as readily as we say a feeling of blue or a feeling of cold." If *Adam Cannot Be Adam*, then Kelli Anne Noftle shows us the middle way, the difficult, liminal space that exists between Adam and Adam, and the feeling that necessitates such a space. "Which adam is the original / which adam is behind the curtain / which adam is the one I am pointing to," Noftle asks. These questions are never so simple as to reveal the wizard behind the curtain; instead, they reveal the system of which that wizard is a function. Noftle carves through the patriarchal structures of love, sex, and religion to remind us that the sense of self is contingent upon the sense of other. *Adam Cannot Be Adam* without the woman—the first, the poet, Kelli Anne Noftle—who makes him so.

JAMES MEETZE, AUTHOR OF *PHANTOM HOUR* AND *DAYGLO*

Kelli Anne Noftle's second collection of poems reveals a brilliant mind observing a shifting subject, the "holographic man," doubled in memory's mirror and in the magical distance of love. Finely wrought and restlessly inquisitive, the poems hover over the point where intimacy "converges with light" in the mind, tinkering with perception, optical illusions, and visual imagery. Noftle's poems are like origami animals, new shapes folded out of the ordinary material of life, offering the reader a transcendent guidebook on "how to see / a picture / made of uncountable / refractions."

MOLLY BRODAK, AUTHOR OF *A LITTLE MIDDLE OF THE NIGHT* AND *BANDIT*

PREVIOUS BOOKS

I Was There For Your Somniloquy
Omnidawn, 2012

ADAM CANNOT BE ADAM

KELLI ANNE NOFTLE

For Maggie —
Thank you for coming
to Malvern! I hope to
read your work soon!

with love !
Kelli

OMNIDAWN PUBLISHING
OAKLAND, CALIFORNIA
2017

Cover Art photo credit: Courtesy Cheim & Read, New York
Jack Pierson, *KNOWEST THOU THE ORDINANCES OF HEAVEN*, 2009,
folded pigment print, dimensions variable.
&
(CYCLOPS), 2010, folded pigment print, dimensions variable.

Cover and interior typefaces: Athelos

Cover design by James Meetze

Interior design by Cassandra Smith

Offset printed in the United States
by Edwards Brothers Malloy, Ann Arbor, Michigan
On 55# Glatfelter B18 Antique
Acid Free Archival Quality Recycled Paper

Library of Congress Cataloging-in-Publication Data

Names: Noftle, Kelli Anne, author.
Title: Adam cannot be Adam / Kelli Anne Noftle.
Description: Oakland, California : Omnidawn Publishing, 2017.
Identifiers: LCCN 2016045482 | ISBN 9781632430335 (pbk. : alk. paper)
Classification: LCC PS3614.O3964 A6 2017 | DDC 811/.6--dc23
LC record available at https://lccn.loc.gov/2016045482

Published by Omnidawn Publishing, Oakland, California
www.omnidawn.com   (510) 237-5472   (800) 792-4957
10 9 8 7 6 5 4 3 2 1
ISBN: 978-1-63243-033-5

CONTENTS

It is, of course, true that the two accounts of the creation of man differ considerably...two Adams, two men, two fathers of mankind, two types, two representatives of humanity...

[they] are not two different people locked in an external confrontation as an "I" opposite a "thou," but one person who is involved in self-confrontation. "I," Adam the first, confront the "I," Adam the second. In every one of us abide two *personae*—

Joseph B. Soloveitchik

I kept you both

in order

to tell the difference

                    Adam the signified
                    Adam the significant

one of you was sleeping

one of you walked

into your sleep

                    Adam the pallbearer
                    Adam the pianist

I kept you both

alive in order

to write in

order to

fold a thing up to be another thing
getting anything to be inside anything

In this story I want both men named Adam.

One Adam works in a textile factory.

The other Adam keeps a jar of ten-year-old water on his shelf.

When we mix pills with whiskey and sleep through dinner.

Adam pounding on my front door.

Adam ignoring my calls.

The jar of water is a gift he tells me.

When we sleep inside a circle of white noise.

Adam wants to have sex all the time.

But the other Adam prefers to dream.

Why there is a cat and sometimes a dog.

Between pleasure and intellect.

When we drink margaritas that smell like Lysol.

Adam's piano takes three months to tune.

The piano tuner's wife is a fortune teller he tells me.

I drive to Adam's house after having sex with Adam.

The fortune teller says he is a crab and he is a goat and I am a ram.

When I see there is something growing in the jar.

Adam tells me I must choose between them.

Rams scare crabs but crabs scare easily.

When the cat brings fleas into my bed.

Between survivor and participant.

Adam says I don't see the big picture.

Why I paint the fireplace white.

The fortune teller says goats and rams will fight like cats and dogs.

That's what you can expect.

Between impartial and fanatic.

And so I ask about the jar.

What is living inside.

Adam says it was a gift and Adam doesn't throw away gifts.

Why the piano makes a linear sound.

Adam is not a replacement for Adam.

Between Genesis and Exodus.

Rams eat goats and goats eat crabs.

What can you expect.

When I am asked to choose facing the hallway.

Between containment and confrontation.

In this story the answer has two faces.

It is a gift.

I dated you both

at the same time

        Adam the taxonomist
        Adam the expelled

one of you pulled

the blinds closed

one of you peeled

an orange

        Adam the raindrop
        Adam the waterfall

I dated both of you

all the time

to construct one

        Adam the righteous
        Adam the dirtbag

I wanted to write

the love of making

is a system

a whole picture

A bag is not exactly
a face from memory.
I started with a bag because
a face is memorable.

A bag is familiar but not
as easily remembered as
an apple core is
not exactly similar to
the peel of an orange.

I started facing
the second day.
The second I started
painting. I opened
the bag. Peeled
the orange. Next to
two daffodils. A jar
for water for daffodils.
A bag with an apple
core is nothing
but a peeled surface.

On the day I started
the daffodils is
the day I looked
at the bag facing
the daffodil and
the daffodil
facing the peel
and so on the same
day the daffodils
face the apple
then the orange
the next day.

I started in exactly
four days. Drawing.
Five days. Surfacing
a look. From looking.

Now flies flying over.

Flies surface
over the opening.
Open as a bag
that is open. As a
face opens. Exactly
familiar with looking.

It is exactly as I look
that every face remembers
starting with a bag.
A surface.
A grounding.

I remember the fifth
day coiled near
the orange peel.
Now an apple
is made bruised
by remembering.

Flies coming that come
the sixth and seventh
days. As they are.
As everything starts
to face me.

On the last day
as I start to stare
I remember. An
orange is not an apple
exactly. Drawn
from memory.

A jar of water
breeds ground.

I wore your jackets

around your houses

                    Adam wool blazer
                    Adam hooded raincoat

I wore out

your names

singing them

in the shower

                    Adam refined
                    Adam organic

I wore

the whole in

every part

I made them contained
within the thing I wrote

Adam pursues me when I stop believing in him.

After an incision, there is a moment of hesitation.

I call him by his real name, Adam the Utilitarian.

When we were poor and ate a can of beans for dinner.

He teaches me everything between quixotic and visionary.

When we watched the cat piss on the floor.

In his dream, someone takes a piece of him.

Adam feeds me the details slowly.

If it tastes like dirt it must be good for me.

Adam sleeps through an emergency.

I wrap the leftovers in a plastic bag.

I call him by his real name, Adam the Covenantal.

When at first the blood looks blue to mock us.

I keep the bag tied tightly.

Adam teaches me everything between.

Vicodin from a vending machine.

When we sat on a crate of soil samples in our living room.

Perfect hole-punched pieces of earth.

I call him by his real name.

Why blood pools somewhere dark in the body.

Between communion and isolation.

Why the bones shaped like a prison cell.

Let us portray this Adam.

The cartoon of his real body.

I turn his disease into my thesis.

Between redemptive and majestic.

In one story, when I was formed.

Pried apart and wrapped with plastic.

I was inconceivable.

Burdened by companionship.

A story of any body.

Called by name.

I held your names

before your bodies

        Adam the loyalist
        Adam the quisling

I held your names

in front of your bodies

and made you dance

        Adam the objective
        Adam the continuous

toward them

dancing like any

thing wanting

its shape back

The night of the election.

When I leave Adam's house in my pajamas.

I drive into the desert to find Adam.

We kiss for the first time in history.

Between kitchen and library.

Adam says I taste like artificial grape jelly.

Between natural and enhanced.

When I close my eyes and his face hovers.

The night we elect our new leader.

I tell Adam it is pomegranate lipstick.

The kiss is a seal or covenant.

I am wearing the pajamas that hang like window drapes.

When I feel Adam circle me.

He takes me to the bedroom.

Why he says I should put no other Adams before him.

The way a circle closes.

Casting our votes behind curtains.

Adam circles his name on the page and points to it.

I say we are finally singular.

Why pomegranate is popular.

In Adam's house we are somebody.

Adam opens my pajamas.

Let us continue now that the other Adam isn't watching.

When I say Adam says.

Let us reap a reward for our labor.

His hands apart.

The artificial fragrance betrays me.

Adam says it reminds me.

Between duty and ecstasy.

The night I choose Adam.

A part is all.

I wrote

apples are oranges

I had a life

outside the garden

        (perspective)

I stacked

the differences

against each other

writing how many

adams it takes

to remember

        (perception)

the hole in the donut
the apple in the dumpling

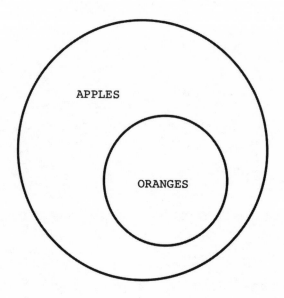

namely because they are much more compatible than the idiom
suggests, furthermore, in many languages, an orange is referred to
as a "golden apple"

I knew

in order to write

to draw points

in a system

the love of naming

must be lost

on Adam

For a time I did not make portraits because I was trying to live in looking, and looking was not to mix itself up with remembering.

Gertrude Stein

Two pictures of a rose in the dark.

Ludwig Wittgenstein

I painted everything exactly as it is. The wood table, lace cloth, peeled orange, wine glass, jar of daffodils in water, paper bag spilling apples. I started with the bag because I saw a face. A face is a good place to begin because it is easy to construct from memory. On the first day I painted the paper bag. I sketched the shape of the bag looking away from the jar with the edges folded open, spilling apples. As I painted the surface of the bag and each of its folds, I saw that the bag was similar to the shape of a face in profile. On the second day, I painted the daffodils as they began to lean, peering into the wine glass. I sketched the orange peel falling away from the orange in one long tendril. I painted it coiling beside the glass and then the pattern of lace beneath the daffodils. I traced their long stems doubling in water. On the sixth and seventh days I painted the part of the bag that looked similar to the mouth of a face and then I drew the opening where apples slipped over the cloth and rolled toward the edge of the table. Every day I came to the table and looked at it and then back at the canvas as the shapes grew more familiar. With each brushstroke I drew closer to understanding what is difficult to forget when looking.

an apple is nothing
but a ripened ovary

all visible
left over

I wanted to make history
less about the garden

what happens after
each minor bruise

reveals a landscape
the insistence of more

what happens when
we act as if

there is no use
in a center

In my story, chips soaked to mush make paper.

The oak touching the window eventually falls through.

I draw a map for Adam on cardboard.

How a childhood bends between ferns, moss, hickory roots.

Why we collapse trees into categories.

Those that cannot self-pollinate or return as a piano bench.

My photo of Adam hugging a Redwood.

Why the ocean is bigger but less scary.

In one story, I cover our faces with palm fronds.

When he tells me to forget about forests.

His cigarettes taste like sand.

How a story collects dust on its surface.

Between pine needles and asphalt.

In this version, I sleep on a stack of wood pallets.

I trace a map of dead telephone poles.

Why the light falls in splinters.

When Adam wakes up, the leaves disappear.

Trees lose their limbs.

Between portraiture and photography.

Whatever the land holds, it wants to uproot.

So I use metal frames, mechanical pencils, vellum from calfskins.

Inspired by unexpected resemblances.

We're born with this one face and isn't it enough.

In his story, the desert is filled with figs.

A painting of the landscape reverses the statement.

Between thirst and indifference.

Between a rock and a featureless place.

On the tenth day, two flies hovered near the wine glass. I painted the glass reflecting the head of the daffodil until the head grew heavier bending down to its reflection. I painted a face over the bag and then a bag over the face remembering how eyes look and are seen almost triangular in profile. On the twenty-second day, I washed the canvas with turpentine. I wanted to start over beginning with the water because water contained in a jar holds shape though water itself is shapeless. I caught one daffodil doubling over and brushing its face against the bag. Flies landed touching the flesh of the orange, its peel, the jar, and more flies landed, tracing an apple's bruise. I scraped my palette knife against the canvas to apply the paint directly. On the thirtieth day I sketched the lace over the table and under the hardened orange peel that coiled near the apple's shape. I painted as the flies came and disappeared into wine or gathered on the orange flesh. Daffodil stems flopped and folded over the bag, petals falling over every surface. The jar, the glass, the skin. Water grew muddy in its container and turned as paint turns on its own, without portraying.

it begins sticky
twinge of infestation
a cutting board stained
with pomegranate seeds
flies circling a jar

civilization is not
a fork or spoon or
a rose
a rose

it begins cloudy
deserted composition
a maggot's rice-like body twitches
flower stems disintegrate in water

preservation is not
a picture or sample or
pattern

it begins turning
curdled at the edges

a hole is not
the end but
a ripening
the luck
of company

a face in the punctured
pie pan

in
his
story
skin
is
a
dis-
ad-
vantage

On the last month, I started with the jar because it stopped reflecting the bag, orange, wine, apple, lace. A jar of water is a breeding ground. It grows around itself in blindness and stops looking or remembering to see. A cloud passed behind and in front of me the moment I began until the second I stopped remembering the table inside the room and all at once it followed my eye as I was following many. Flies overhead landed over and over trying to touch everything. I painted this motion from the center of the room starting with the table and following the swarm. Fly into fly as each touched down repeatedly with emphasis. In a cloud, I followed the brush in my hand pushing it over the surface. Back and forth continuously.

the painting is

a trash can

what we need

to shed

gets abandoned

on the surface

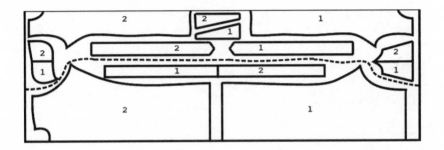

when cutting pieces from the same cloth, with respect to table surface, there are three directions: face up, face down, and face to face

what is a thing
which progresses
is it less splendid
than the absence
of advancement

here in Adam's house
I am moving
my hands over
the walls
my feet across
linoleum

it is dancing
is it more
certain than stance

sound without
understanding
a stutter

the interstitial
movements

a home
that collapses
from progress is
more insistent
with words

the momentum
of saying we will
and we should be
remembered advancing

equally without
a hitch

to keep time
we clap
our hands
split the bills
call it progress

it begins inside
a wall
a mail slot
the setting for
embedded pigeons
a rotting roof
a buckled floor-
board begins
to stammer
a fireplace
buried half bird
half brick

Adam blames
the house
the history
of houses swollen
between other
buildings under
water a city
is still
a concrete
thing he says

a cloud
tethered to
other clouds
makes curtains

In this story, she thinks about dyeing her hair.

As a painted scrim to indicate scenery.

Why Adam says he will not cover his head.

If he is the image of god.

Adam questions whether the carpet matches the drapes.

To indicate suspicion her hair has been painted.

If their story is bound or contains a partition.

But Adam wants to know if the carpet matches.

Why we start in the middle and work toward the beginning.

Her eyelash, freckle, birthmark, dimple.

Why shutters shut and shutters shut and also.

In this story of holes, a fault in the fabric.

When we ask what is pictured behind the curtain.

Pockmark, chipped tooth, varicose vein.

Why the painted windows cannot seal the bedroom.

If she is the image of Adam, posing inside the photo booth.

Why the sound of the camera becomes tolerable.

Shutters shut and shutters shut.

Why we say they are cut from the same cloth.

To indicate resemblance, similarity, familial.

The length of her hair in a shapeless veil.

Shutters open.

When sunlight rakes the floorboards, bookshelves, kitchen sink.

Adam wraps her neck with cashmere.

In this story, the picture is the curtain.

A space between door and floor pooling light.

there's nothing new
about sincerity
see Adam
stand between
a kitchen and living
room touching
our curtain
hung to split
the spaces

says I don't
says he knows

how to use
the word
irony correctly

its dictionary
definition too
often displaced
in door's absence

I pull back
the drape
he pinched
closed he claims
it keeps heat
on the one
side how does
that work I don't
do physics
but surely this
is built-in

ironic division

Adam prefers
correcting me

the gist of
so sorry
sincerely

from the bottom
I'm mistaken
my misuse
our bad apple

what's it called
when you repeat
a word
too many times

misleading

whatsitcalled
when we go
bankrupt

bad luck

try to decipher

which adam is here

which adam is the name Adam

which adam is the portrait

which adam is the idea behind the word adam

which adam is the original

which adam is behind the curtain

which adam is her

which adam is the one I am pointing to

and away from

I knew him as intimately as I knew my own image in a mirror. In other words, I knew him only in relation to myself. Yet, on those terms, I knew him perfectly. At times, I thought I was inventing him as I went along, however, you will have to take my word for it that we existed.

Angela Carter

The face itself is redundancy.

Gilles Deleuze

A picture of the junkyard at midnight. Shattered windshields
heaped against a wilderness. The desert won't keep track of
time but needs massive amounts of energy, spread across the
badlands to appear casual. I've been wondering about you in three
dimensions. Glass, plastic, metal. I've been wondering if holograms
are photographs that never die. Somehow the image gets trapped
inside. See? I'm in the empty lot with my door ajar. I'm tilting my
credit card, looking for your face in a moving bird. We are only
inches from a future. The adequate amount of space for desolation
is predetermined. Here, a supermarket from this angle, a salvage
yard on the horizon, twelve locusts, a jar of honey. What makes
you different from the other? A composition compelling in its near
obscurity? I'm not even allowed to talk about your ghost—

as in holograms

I cannot
bisect him
to discern
a separateness

image of the apple

cut in half
illuminated
halved in

fourths I ask
how such portions
remain graceful

if I am
with him
contained
in the blur

bathed then
burdened
and bathed again
by light

then all
I have to do
for the most part
is refocus

That space between the door and floor where fig leaves blew in.
It was Adam who said nothing is predestined, shaking the jar of
water like a snow globe. Rotating white noise samples, convinced
our machine lacked the "desert" setting, he pried the sounds apart
until they split. The tear became a hole that we could sleep in. At
night the sky burned darker near its edges and I was reminded of
a lesson I'd learned: the artist makes his wound visible on canvas.
We discussed Bosch's *Garden of Earthly Delights*. The far right
panel, that guy with the flute in his ass. And Cezanne's apples?
The problem with a still life. Ripeness becoming rot. It was later
I discovered the word adam has twofold signification. Red earth
combines the notion of man's material origin with a connotation
of the ground color from which he was formed. I dreamed myself
along diverging narratives, trapped between a collapsible space.
It occurred to me the static he preferred formed a landscape that
could be reproduced, even without the original. Regardless of the
rift in etymologies, Adam was just a guy who said he loved me
with a gap in his teeth. Now more than ever I want to write about
landfills and junkyards and leave the dirt piling up around my
ears. Even if I paint the fireplace white even if I close my eyes to
differences I don't care about his autographs I want fig leaves to fill
the entire kitchen I want to look at photographs without comparing
myself to music to the mark a palette knife makes scraping against
the surface to a refinery to a freezer burn a ruddy face an engine to
a doppelganger to "mankind" to that golden apple paradox,

in this sentence

meaning collapses

I fold

his name

between pages

I separate

the counterfeit

from the living

with an invisible

curtain

this way

Adam cannot

be adam

and remind us

beam → mirror → apple → recording →

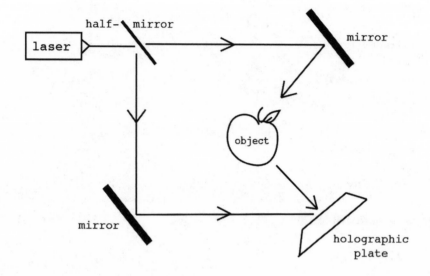

smash a hologram of an apple into tiny bits and you can still see the whole apple in each individual piece

the holographic man

does not double
or represent

but moves on
his own

a specter
in periphery

I circle his image
in the flesh

identify parts
in person

the history
of recorded light
is a permanent
reflection

Common examples include seeing animals or people in clouds or hearing hidden messages on records played in reverse. Sometimes the brain is almost too good at recognizing faces. Like that time in Berkeley I kissed a woman who looked exactly like Adam. You can't develop a photographic memory but you can reconstruct the rest of the head even if two facial features are the only attributes visible. A few beers later, the modulation of light, your hair is different, you've gained weight. The simplistic drawing of three circles and a line on the side of a building—whose smile is that? To understand holography, one can think of it as similar to recording whereby a sound field is encoded in such a way that it can be reproduced later without the presence of the original. Remembering is repetition. That woman looked like no one I knew, yet she was familiar. Remembering is confusion. Lines of graffiti. Despite the complete lack of resemblance to a real human face, I recognized someone. What's that called? A highly evolved survival trait? To render a faceless apparition, one must capture both the immaterial and the palpable. A skull in a rosebud. Jesus Christ in a grilled cheese. Try to decipher which Adam in history. Holography is also a metaphor some physicists use to describe our ability to store memories in the universe. Forget the brain. Some facts face the wrong way and so we have to twist them. Sometimes we must face the music going backwards.

This is the part when we sit in a junkyard.

To alter the picture, I change the lens.

We are in the junkyard sitting and sifting.

When light strikes, it scatters the particles.

Adam sifts through disconnected images.

It's a well-regulated scatter.

Why lenses articulate details.

Adam crouches inside a forgotten building.

It's a fuzzy picture.

Why concrete eventually crumbles.

Adam uses my shirt to clear the dust.

Poked holes make a pattern of interference.

Why taking the lenses away produces a hologram.

In a yard for discarded furniture.

The senses are the lenses.

When Adam peers through the chain link.

Dust cannot be removed.

Let us take away the appearance of the junkyard.

Let us try to abandon structure.

Why we are consumed but not ruined.

For instance, within the blur is the actual image.

When we try to hide Adam from Adam.

The senses interfere.

The way leftovers get distributed, spread out.

Adam covering his face with his hands.

For instance, if you sift between sentences.

Let us frame this Adam or the other.

Suspended as a particle in a shaft of light.

Let us name his reflection before it scatters.

In this story a story of difference.

How light fills the abandoned structure.

A story dislocated, interrupted.

The mouth replaced by a lens.

Today everything exists to end in a photograph.

Susan Sontag

The camera relieves us of the burden of memory.

John Berger

She uses a bottle
and a scouring pad.

These are the first
measures of removal.

The first half erased
from a two-sided story—

You can't have both, he says, moving
into focus

                 between rubbish and resource

                 between filament and tapestry

to blot
out one part
and still hold
the picture

she knows in order
to articulate
their differences
painting a portrait
is almost impossible

so she shoots the canyon, sprained ankle, frayed carpet, chewed ink
pens, yellow slicker, month old figs wrapped in paper,

as if by framing
fragments she might
emphasize

knees pressed
to her chest
zooming to find

the pattern of rain
inside a grocery bag

her subject flattened

Hold still

she says, snapping

                              between chain link and picket

                              between symbolic and imaginary

a photograph
of Adam
          in ruins

does it not resemble, does it repeat
a likeness

asked not to blink   (for the length of the exposure)
he stares
into cracks
of the building   (she insists)

to imitate himself
advancing the image—

his cheek pressed to
a broken window

she says: *I want you to look*

away from me
and into

the camera

as if by focusing
on one point
between middle and ending

she shoots the filmy bathtub ring, a month's worth of apple cores
saved in plastic bags, aims at his name in the canyon wall where
she scraped the letters with a shard of glass

A

D

A

M

can he see
the aperture widening

between repetition and insistence

between obsession and daydream

yes

closing

the door

opening

his raincoat

she aims at silly phrases personal hatreds superstitions private
pleasures she captures neurosis indulgence disappointment she
drops his slicker onto concrete watches rain funnel into his boots
holds the camera up
to his face and facing him takes the picture

shutters   *shut and shutters*   *shut and so   shutters*

        shut and so

                                        and

                                                also

between plastic and graphic

between compulsion and deviation

I don't want to do it, he says one day, moving
out of frame.

You don't have to

she says after

the image is

already recorded

after all

there is no such thing as repetition
and really how can there be

See:

between tiles on their bathroom floor, she used a bottle of rubbing
alcohol and a hard yellow sponge. The last room she cleaned
before moving. The last apartment on the right with the yellow
stucco and climbing ivy with the urine stained carpet with the
green shutters and broken mail slot

other Adams
bring mattresses desk lamps litter boxes bookshelves

others fill the space
saying

you can roll paint over one
thing to cover another
but you can't stop
shifting between

repetition insistence repetition insistence

she knows
so far
between *us*
the only sound
familiar is
the camera

how

       sssssssshuttttterssss

          sssssssssshuttt

   and   fall

          open

       even

              though

    we stoop

         inside

      the viewfinder

                 lowering

        our heads

        in lamplight

  surely mercy

surely

a reflection

        pulled into curved glass

converges with light

           surely we both

find his face on the same side

walk in

       a crowd
               again
               one
    day

and now

        and now let us

            follow   let resemblance

                fall

          into resemblance

hinging on

                  emphasis

       how to see

a picture

      made of uncountable

         refractions

between pseudo-presence

lenses wrapped
with old socks

newspapers covered in dried
tomato seeds

between one token and the next

toothbrush on the back of the toilet

cigarette butts in pie tins

she uses prolonged exposures, tricks the lens for several hours,
changes the color of midnight, aims at contours without blinking,
holds open the sky until it burns

an effigy

between

two

possible

faces

SEE: figure SEE: Adam SEE: ground SEE:

:::::::container:::::::

orange peel
cocktail napkin
pillowcase
grocery bag

a jar

of water

bending   light

on the window sill

A story requires resemblance and the results are bound to include recognizable sounds in their totality as horns and windmills and the story is "ours"

Lyn Hejinian

as soon as we
start over
with an image
of a water faucet
we picture how it
falls dripping

a sleep machine
set to waterfalls
rushes us into
stories we recognize
as dreams when we
follow Adam
following raindrops
counting them as
a metronome
on a piano bench

measuring narratives
we divide
pages to bind
books to fit
boxes to remember
the room grows
hollow when a story
stops here
and begins
again portraying

the picture of water
or the hallow
sound of it
falling over
hands we want
to wash
this image
into memory
wholly ours
to assemble

for every meaning

there must be

two names

for every experience

the image

will show us how

to let go of it

                   (shapeless)

but the skin

of a dream

is resilient

Remember the story when Adam races the rain clouds doubling.

Why we ask *what is cloudiness, is it a lining, is it a roll.*

Between facial features or animal bodies seen in cumulus.

A painting demonstrates the sky's unnameable change.

When we ask how an orphan droplet becomes ten thousand.

Remember watered-down pigments drip off the canvas.

Rain beating against a metal door is a type of white noise.

Remember some characters tear holes in the story's lining.

Why we can see both Adams simultaneously.

A cloud is made of crystals but shaped like an anvil.

Remember one Adam's suffering is another's solitude.

A photograph captures the funnel cloud advancing.

When we gather reflections before the shadow absorbs them.

Let us interpret the story as symbols on a weather map.

Between evidence and memory.

Pointing to the wind pointing to the sound of windmills.

Cloudiness as a lining as a blueprint as a thought blooms.

Let us occupy each part of a two-fold confusion.

Between crystallized and occluded.

Cloud subsuming cloud, splitting sky or casting cover.

Between points in an endless folding.

what we need

we leave

to holes

left open

9: The opening epigraph is from Rabbi Joseph B. Soloveitchik's book-length essay, *The Lonely Man of Faith*, and refers to the two biblical accounts of the creation of man that appear in Genesis 1 and 2. In the New International Version Bible, written in Genesis 1, "God created mankind in his own image, in the image of God he created them; male and female he created him." This Adam is instructed to "be fruitful and increase in number" and "have dominion over all the earth." In Genesis 2 there is another story of creation: "Then the Lord God formed a man from the dust of the ground and breathed into his nostrils the breath of life, and man became a living being." This second version of Adam is placed in the garden to "work and take care of it." Soloveitchik acknowledges that many critics believe the two narratives are attributed to different traditions and sources; however, he believes that both versions represent two personality types in each one of us (the utilitarian and covenantal).

11, 17, 23: The italicized text in each poem is from Gertrude Stein's "Portraits and Repetitions" in *Lectures in America*.

18-19: "Adam the Utilitarian" and "Adam the Covenantal" as well as "Let us portray this Adam" are adapted from and make reference to concepts about dual Adams found in Soloveitchik's *The Lonely Man of Faith*.

29: The final stanzas echo the phrase "act so that there is no use in a centre," from Gertrude Stein's poem "Rooms" in *Tender Buttons*.

38: The first lines are adapted from "A thing without progress is more splendid than a thing which progresses," from Stein's *Picasso*.

41, 64, 68: The phrase "shutters shut and shutters shut and so" is borrowed from Stein's poem about Picasso, "If I Told Him."

41: "Why the sound...becomes tolerable," echoes Roland Barthes's *Camera Lucida*, "the only thing that I tolerate...when I am photographed, is the sound of the camera."

43-44: "There's nothing new about sincerity" is borrowed from Anthony Robinson's "A few notes from a New Sincerist," which was published in the July 2005 blog entry of Geneva Convention Archives. Ideas about the usage of the word *irony* also make reference to Robinson's blog.

45: Language in "try to decipher" was inspired by Joshua Clover's essay on language poetry, "The Rose of the Name," published by *Fence* in the Spring 1998 issue. The poem makes reference to Stein's "a rose is a rose is a rose" in Clover's words: "try to puzzle out which is the word 'rose,' which indicates the idea of the *rose*, and which stands for a particular rose..."

48: Lines on holograms reference a description found at www.explainthatstuff.com/holograms: "Holograms are a bit like photographs that never die," and "photos that have somehow got trapped inside glass, plastic, or metal."

50: "Red earth combines the notion of man's material origin with a connotation of the ground color from which he was formed" is borrowed from newadvent.org, specifically the encyclopedia entry on "Adam."

51: "Smash a hologram..." is a phrase adapted from a description about how holograms work, found at www.explainthatstuff.com/holograms. The diagram is a combination of various drawings on "how to make a hologram" from the same website, as well as www.technotif.com/create-hologram, http://www.hgt-global.com/hologram_recording_process.html, and in *The Holographic Universe* by Michael Talbot.

54: "Common examples include..." is adapted from the Wikipedia entry on Pareidolia and makes reference to the article "Pareidolia: Why we see faces in the hills, the Moon, and toasties," published by www.bbc.com/news/magazine on May 31, 2013.

"Remembering is repetition" and "remembering is confusion" are borrowed from Stein's "Portraits and Repetitions" in *Lectures in America*.

This poem also references a Wikipedia entry on "how holography works," comparing holography to a sound recording: "whereby a sound field created by vibrating matter like musical instruments or vocal cords, is encoded in such a way that it can be reproduced later without the presence of the original vibrating matter."

"Holography is also a metaphor..." makes reference to Karl Pribram's holographic brain theory, examined in *The Holographic Universe* by Michael Talbot.

55-56: Concepts and language throughout this poem echo Karl Pribram's holographic brain theory, specifically from an interview Jeffery Mishlove conducted with Pribram from the series "Thinking Aloud."

61: The line "between symbolic and imaginary" makes reference to terms found in Jacques Lacan's psychoanalytic theory, and is for my friend Eric.

66: The italicized text is from Gertrude Stein's "Portraits and Repetitions" in *Lectures in America*.

71: Describing a photograph as a "pseudo-presence" is borrowed from Susan Sontag's *On Photography*.

77: The italicized text is from Stein's poem "Food" in *Tender Buttons*.

Again, some of the language here echoes Clover's writing in his essay "The Rose of the Name," in particular a "two-fold confusion" found in language poetry. Clover writes "confusions of kind bloom like roses and roses and roses, each with fold on fold, folding in on itself indefinitely."

Acknowledgments

Gracious thanks to the editors of *The Laurel Review*, *Manor House Quarterly*, *New Orleans Review*, *The Offending Adam*, and *Souvenir*, where some of these poems first appeared (in slightly altered form). I am endlessly grateful for dear friends who read, edited, listened, encouraged and offered inspiration throughout the writing of this manuscript: Eric Taggart, James Meetze, Andrew Wessels, Elena Karina Byrne, Emily Jayne Motzkus, Dorota Orechwa, and my heart, Brad Thomas. Enormous thanks to Rusty Morrison who helped me shape this work into the book it wanted to be and to everyone at Omnidawn for their tireless efforts and dedication.

A big thanks to Jack Pierson for permission to use the cover images and to James Meetze for the cover design, guidance, and unparalleled support.

photo by: Brad Thomas

Kelli Anne Noftle is a visual artist, musician, poet, and business manager who divides her time between Los Angeles and San Diego. Poems and music can be found at www.kelliannenoftle.com